CARDOZO
N

ERIC GILL

Further Thoughts by
an Apprentice

# MR ERIC GILL

## Further Thoughts by an Apprentice

DAVID KINDERSLEY

Cambridge 1990
CARDOZO KINDERSLEY EDITIONS
UITGEVERIJ DE BUITENKANT

Added to this facsimile of
the Ward Ritchie presentation of 1967
is an attempt to provide an appreciation
of the validity of Gill's views
and work today.

Mr Eric Gill © Ward Ritchie Press 1967
New matter © David Kindersley 1982
New impression 1990 published by
Cardozo Kindersley Editions
152 Victoria Road
Cambridge CB4 3DZ

British Library Cataloguing in Publication Data
Kindersley, David
Eric Gill: further thoughts by an apprentice.–New ed.
1. English engravings. Gill, Eric 1882–1940
I Title
769.92
ISBN 0 950194654 5 4

Text paper supplied by William Sommerville & Son P.L.C.
Cover paper is Charisma Haze supplied by Robert Horne
Printed by Black Bear Press, Cambridge

TO PETRA

ARTHUR ERIC ROWTON GILL was born on the twenty-second of February 1882, the second child of a family of twelve. He died at the age of only 58 after an operation for lung cancer.

Towards the end of his life he received many honours. He was elected an Honorary Associate of the Royal Institute of British Architects, an Associate of the Royal Academy, an Honorary Doctor of Law at Edinburgh University and his was among the first appointments to the distinction of Designer for Industry. That Mr Gill accepted the Honorary Associateship offered by the Royal Institute of British Architects is fair considering his earlier education in the offices of the architect to the Ecclesiastical Commissioners where he learned draughtsmanship which stood him in good stead when later he had his own clients to deal with – but his A.R.A. might justifiably have been refused by him because he had on one occasion been denied entry to a Royal Academy dinner due to his attire, he was wearing his own kind of smart evening smock. As a Designer for industry there can be no dispute. It is often forgotten that type designers are Industrial Designers 'par excellence'.

It is not surprising to me that there is a revival of interest in Eric Gill – the man who thought and then 'made his think'. Thoughting and making have become two quite separate activities and young craftsmen don't like this dichotomy. Gill has much to say to all of us who try to run small workshops making things that people want. Perhaps this is the point, he believed in the making of 'things' that people wanted. The industrial world, for its very existence, must make things that people buy and the bigger the sale the more sameness – the more sameness the less quality engendered. The less appreciation of quality the more trivia – the more trivia – the more boredom – the more boring the things around us are the more desire to have things made personally. Perhaps we are reaching this point at last – at least there are many makers of things today working in two's or threes. In a very real sense Eric Gill saw the human need for making, and he saw very clearly that a society for the want of anything better had to buy the things made for the profit of share holders rather than the things that might otherwise be made for them by craftsmen.

An industrial designer is judged by his ability to satisfy the greedy machines that have to spew out

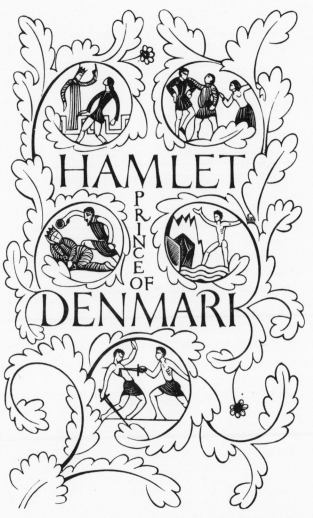

Title page from *Hamlet*
Limited Editions Club, New York 1933

objects that nobody needs but which the public has been taught to want. A good craftsman works for clients that specify quite clearly what they need. The very starting point for a craftsman is human – his market is never a mass market. A designer is often used by machines even if he thinks otherwise. Whereas the true craftsman regards computers and machines merely as tools and I'm sure that were Gill alive today he would be enjoying the new digital typography.

Eric Gill realised that man needed to use his hands in a skilful way – that is standing back and thinking – thinking all around the problem until something satisfactory as a solution evolved. It always seemed to me that he had that which he was going to make very clearly in his mind.

It is important to be trained and it's never too early to start. This is accepted by us all if, for instance, you happen to be a musician or a ballet dancer. But it has always seemed unfair to me that other talents for some extraordinary reason seem less obvious to us. In the case of the musician or ballet dancer, your education is rightly subordinated to your art/craft, indeed such education as you glean is probably deepened and enriched by your training. If you discover your vocation too late you will probably be sent to an art school. The shallowness of such is reflected in the multitude of subjects to which you are exposed, and in the

# GILL SANS

LETTERS ARE SIGNS FOR SOUNDS. SIGNS FOR numbers of other things like the sign for a dollar may in practice be included, though they are not strictly letter signs used in Algebra). Letters are not Pictures or re-presentations. Picture writing or hieroglyphics are not

LETTERS FROM OUR POINT OF VIEW; and tho' our letters, our signs for sounds, may be shown to be derived from picture writing, such derivation is so much of the dim and distant past as to concern us no

LONGER. LETTERS ARE NOT PIC-tures or representations. They are more or less abstract forms. Hence they have peculiar attraction for the 'mystical mug' called man. More than most things, Letters allow him to Chinese) the high place of calligraphy and the inscription. Among the Chinese good writing is more highly honoured even than

CONSIDER BEAuty with-out fear of what the Home Secretary may think or do. Art and morals are inextri-cably mixed, but here is an

ART FREER from ad-ulteration than most arts. Hence among a highly cultured & rat-ional people (like the

painting is with us, as highly per-haps as we reverence & look up to

A GREAT BOILER OF SOAP

# Hague and Gill

PRINTERS

PIGOTTS, HIGH WYCOMBE

Type Specimen
Hague & Gill, Pigotts 1933

products of the students which are generally absurd and trivial. Society has created grand institutions to help foist all this chaos on the public who have to be rich to buy the current 'status symbol'. 'What's it all blooming well for' was Eric Gill's reaction to all this art nonsense and a good many other ills of our day.

I think he was a very disillusioned man when he died – the war had started, raids on London were nightly occurrences and he had believed that somehow war would not happen. But we live now in a completely different era – the worst has happened and no doubt there is more to come. The last few nights have seen rioting youths in some of our major cities. What education did they endure and how is it that nothing worthwhile doing occurs to them. Could it be that the Educational Authorities have not realised that education is for leisure and not work. The western world in which we live today is a world of plenty certainly compared to the thirties. It really ought to be possible to help the young, emerging into the adult world which now offers them no work and will increasingly offer less and less employment – to look for the benefits of leisure. This at least would be a more worthwhile exercise than education for 'form filling'.

Our great debt to Eric Gill is firstly for the marvellous quality of his line on the wood block

# UNEMPLOYMENT

¶ IT IS absolutely necessary to have principles, that is things that come first, the foundations of the house. What we want to know is: what principles of common sense are relevant to the matter of human work.

Unemployment. An engraving as title page.
Pamphlet printed by Hague & Gill, Pigotts 1933.
Price 1/–

and the relation of designs to text so perfectly integrated. Secondly for his completeness as a man who survived as an individual and an eccentric in a world of rigid outlook. Thirdly as a writer on almost any subject that imprisoned the minds of his contemporaries. Fourthly his bravery as a carver in a world of abstract sculpture. Last but certainly not least his devout belief in the Catholic church which I must say often did its best to dampen his enthusiasm for life.

# MR ERIC GILL

*Recollections of*
DAVID KINDERSLEY

I HAD BEEN WORKING for some months with a firm of Italian marble-carvers. There we put into stone or marble the statuary and portrait heads that were modelled in clay by respectable Royal Academicians. Indeed there was more of our work in The Royal Academy Annual Exhibitions than that carved by the sculptors themselves. In those days it was the accepted method. Sculptors did not carve stone they modelled in clay for casting or for replica in stone or marble.

I had just begun to read Mr Gill's books and the dishonesty of this method of working, both from the standpoint of the artist and the material, began to cause me some uneaseness. I found someone writing about making things in stone and emphasizing that a thing made in stone must be a stone thing—just as a thing made in wood must be a wood thing. It was not right to make a thing in clay and then copy it in stone. Different materials work differently. Realizing that I was no longer satisfied working as the

Italians did, I sought an interview with Mr Gill hoping to work with and be taught by him.

Frequently, later, I overheard my father saying, in hushed tones, "I apprenticed my son to the sculptor, Eric Gill." Admittedly, he did put down the small premium when the time came, but the truth is that people such as my father never knew people like Mr Gill. If he had he would certainly not have encouraged me to apprentice to him. My father was a stock-broker in the City of London. We had a pleasant house in the country where we spent our time playing tennis or golf and having very heated arguments about politics and religion. This background, and an English public school education was in sharp contrast to the new life I was to experience when I arrived, aged 18, at Mr Gill's workshop.

A letter had been written on my behalf by a mutual acquaintance, but Mr Gill had replied that he could not take on anyone else. Undaunted, I came to Mr Gill's. Fortunately he was there and would see me.

The one thing I dared not confess to him was the work I was doing with the Italians. Having read his books I thought this would be enough to end the interview! He told me he would be unable to take me as he had all the helpers he needed—indeed he was expecting another to

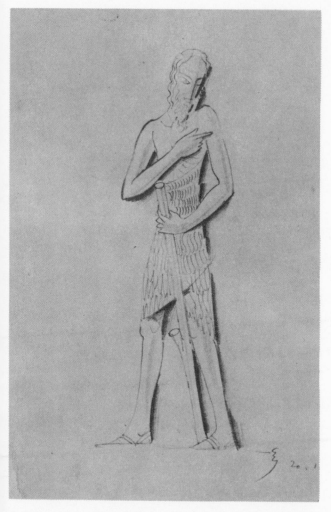

It was my very great privilege to be allowed to work on the back of this carving of St. John Baptist. To a critic, Mr Gill would often say, "If the Almighty had made us in stone instead of flesh and blood this is how we would have been—obeying different laws".

How fortunate for St. Johns College, Oxford, to have one of his very best carvings.

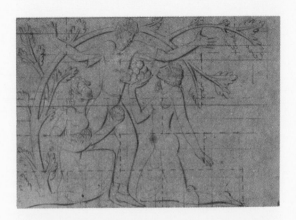

*Mr Gill made many drawings for the entrance to Dorset House in Gloucester Place, London. For reasons of economy and a certain lack of courage on the part of the Board of Directors, these two "Washing" and "Eating" alone found their way into stone. They belonged to a set of four which included "Drinking" and "Sleeping"—all perfectly reasonable activities for a block of apartments! Mr Gill and I worked many days alone on these carvings. Due to a complaint from an elderly spinster living opposite, a London "bobby" had to climb the scaffolding to ascertain that Mr Gill was not masquerading as a woman!*

NOS
AUTEM
POPULUS
EIUS·ET·OVES
PASCUAE·EIUS

CONSTITUISTI·EUM
SUPER·OPERA
MANUUM
TUARUM

*Designs for the two panels to be executed in Hopton-Wood stone at either end of the 30' 0" figure of "Man being touched by the hand of God". The right hand panel was left entirely in the hands of Laurie Cribb, Mr Gill's chief assistant for many years. The work was completed and fixed in The League of Nations building in 1937. Mr Gill wrote to me asking for my help ". . . if Muss & Hit will allow us to complete".*

*All the drawings for The League of Nations building at Geneva, including careful details to the packers and shippers, are in the William Andrews Clark Memorial Library.*

*Sketch for Blue Horton stone. Stone sun dial now at the William Andrews Clark Memorial Library.*

*Portland stone garden roller. Simple everyday objects of use were made in the workshop at Pigotts. Everything was considered for its use and carefully inscribed or carved.*

*Hopton-Wood stone alphabet painted within the "Vee-cut" cut for Graham Carey.*

*Raised letters in stone, bought by the Victoria and Albert Museum. Very near sans serif and with little difference between the weight of vertical and horizontal strokes.*

start work in the coming week. Then he asked the question, "What are you doing with yourself now?"

There was a simple straight forwardness in Mr Gill which I was to realise ever more forcibly later on. But at this first brief encounter it was impossible not to respond truthfully. I explained, expecting that all was now lost, that I had been trying to learn about masonry and carving (I did not know one could do such things in Art Schools) and that these Italians had wanted an assistant. At once Mr Gill changed his mind. "I think if you come back in a month I can take you. You see the chap that is coming has been to an Art School and I don't think he will last here more than a month." My elation knew no bounds.

I asked him, "What should I do in the coming weeks?" He answered, "Make something, it doesn't matter what it is, but make something that you know about. Make a wireless set if that is something you understand."

I went to Italy, and I suppose I saw the Trajan Column and its inscription, though I must confess I did not remember it! This perhaps was a stroke of luck as I came to lettering completely fresh when I started work with Mr Gill. Indeed, Mr Gill did not fully share his contemporaries' enthusiasm for the pure Roman alphabet with its subtle inclining counters and pointed M's & N's.

My first job for Mr Gill, apart from getting the tea, sweeping up and lighting fires, was the making of a huge capital 'L'. It was masoned out of a solid block some four feet in height and projected in relief about five inches. Then an 'S' of the same size. These letters were a part of the name Bentall's, which was a large shopping centre on the outskirts of London. These letters were carved in the workshop and we went away to carve Mr Bentall's coat-of-arms on the shop corner '*in situ*', together with various small carvings supporting the windows. The coat-of-arms was very big—one could get one's hands right into the folds of the 'mantling' and still hammer away. The crest surmounting the helm was a leopard and due to the nature of stone, it was necessary that the tail of the beast was attached to the torse around the top of the helm. The tail could not possibly be carved curling upwards as required by Mr Bentall. There was a very violent Mr Bentall accusing Mr Gill of dishonouring his family by making his leopard look like a cur, Mr Gill offering to add some more spots to his leopard. This all happened on a busy traffic-ridden street, it being the only position from which to view the carving.

The building was in process of construction,

with brick-layers, carpenters, plumbers and electricians everywhere. One morning they were gone. It was a strike. Quite without thinking we had let slip to a bricklayer what we were paid by Mr Gill. Our pay was small indeed and I suppose they thought that we were undercutting them. The senior one of us telephoned Mr Gill. By a stroke of luck Mr Gill was an honorary member of the union that had caused the bother and soon the trouble was smoothed over.

Those of us who were single never gave money a thought. I think it is true to say that all of us would have worked for Mr Gill without payment or, at the most, for our board and lodging. Indeed on one occasion, when money was short, we all immediately offered to work without payment. The work, and the doing of it as well as we could, was our sole aim. There were difficulties for those who were married and had families, and I do think more money should have been found for them. Grumbles rightly were to be heard from the wives but the work was not affected. We worked all hours, late into the night when necessary.

Mr Gill's method of teaching lettering, if he ever did teach (you must bear in mind that lettering was everywhere and inscriptions were continuously being cut in the workshop), was to ask you to draw an alphabet as you thought the letters should be. Having done this Mr Gill corrected it, saying, "Here we make an 'A' like this" or "a 'B' like that." He always spoke quietly and he never told one not to do anything he was doing, but would say, with quiet authority, "You make it like this," and more often than not he anchored the thing in your mind with an appropriate and amusing anecdote. In this way one could compare the letters made without knowledge and experience and their improved version rendered with his deft skill.

After such an experience and having re-drawn my alphabet again and once more having had it corrected, the time came for me to cut my first alphabet. This would be in Hopton-Wood stone, an Oolitic Limestone very hard and capable of being polished like marble. Its later widespread use was very largely due to the publicity resulting from Mr Gill. It could be very precise and sharp, but its great quality was that perfection of incision could only be procured with difficulty. Hopton-Wood consists of minute shell fossils and the stone within the fossil and around them is soft by comparison with the shell itself. In consequence, all the time, one must be on the watch regulating the angle of cut—steeper if hard—shallower if soft. This inevitably makes for concentration from the letter-cutter and, providing he has a good letter-form in his mind's eye, the very best work usually results from work in this stone. You were told in Mr Gill's workshop that if you could carve letters in Hopton-Wood stone you would be able to carve letters in anything. Hopton-Wood stone is a constant challenge to the letter-cutter and I believe it played its own part in Mr Gill's development as a letterer.

After I had finished my alphabet in Hopton-Wood stone and had carefully painted the letters in light red and grey black I went on to carve a small inscription. Mistakes always had to remain. Mr Gill never allowed an apprentice to put an error right by any means whatever. For example, if a small piece of stone chipped out of the edge of a letter it was a chip for all time. I think he felt that the letter should be a faithful rendering of that which one had in the mind's eye. That the letter suffered damage by accident or carelessness was of little importance compared to cutting a letter that was ill-conceived. To thicken the stroke of a letter even slightly to do away with the chip would be creating something false and quite different from the original intention. He believed that most mistakes resulted from a lack of attention and encouraged us to concentrate on what we had conceived in our mind.

In cutting my first inscription I remember

carefully carving serifs on the inside 'vee' of several 'M's. Just as I was about to cut yet another 'M' Laurie Cribb, Mr Gill's chief assistant, spotted my mistake and sent me to see Mr Gill. I was worried about the master's reaction but I saw a way out of the difficulty. If I continued to put serifs in the same place on the rest of the 'M's in the inscription my mistake would appear not as a mistake but as an intention. Mr Gill lost no time in telling me that this would not be fair or right and since I was aware of my mistake it would be dishonest to continue. This pervasive adherence to honesty had a lasting impression upon anyone that worked with him.

Mr Gill explained in great detail how one should hold the chisel when cutting. He attached great importance to economy of effort so that there would be no distraction of attention from the project at hand. We were not to achieve a cut by any pressure from the hand that held the tool, but rather alter the angle of the tool in relation to the surface of the stone to achieve a deep or shallow cut and to drive the tool with the momentum of the letter-cutter's dummy, rather than hit it hard.

All stone arrived at Pigotts workshop in random sawn slabs and before the smallest inscription could be begun we would cope the stone away from the larger slab. Always a somewhat hair-raising task, but Mr Gill drew our attention to the change of "ring" that occurred when the stone was ready to come away. Then all the edges were squared and carefully pointed, clawed, chiselled and rubbed. The surface would be rubbed with finer and finer stones until it began to glow like an eggshell. Beyond this point one seldom went since a shine on the surface would detract from the inscription.

Mr Gill's workshops at Pigotts, amongst the beechwoods of Buckinghamshire, were converted from fine 18th century barns surrounding the farmyard. A pigsty was built of brick in the centre of the yard and their muck hummed and enriched the air—a little too much on a hot day. Mr Gill had his workshop and drawing office on the opposite side to us. At one end were the house and cottages. At the other, The Hague & Gill Press, operated in a long low outhouse.

Those that worked in "The Press" were superior beings compared to us stone masons. They did not, except at rare times, seem to be as busy—always a sign of superiority. Occasionally we were raided and insults were hurled at us. We, quite frankly, resented them and felt that we earned money which they in turn squandered. I'm sure there was little truth in our limited vision, but it seemed that they always obtained what they wanted from Mr Gill, whilst we had little to comfort us materially. For example our fire for the winter was usually out, but it was fun collecting wood from the surrounding beech woods. Laurie Cribb would arrive trailing dead branches behind him —muttering always about the difficulties of an ever increasing family and the Roman Church that made this inescapable. Laurie was certainly the finest letter-cutter of all time. He seemed to have learned all there was to know years before—his work had become instinctive. The exact opposite of his master, it seemed that he could only work in an unholy mess. He drew out his inscriptions apparently without any certainty of where the letters should be and rubbed them out with spit and thumb. Carving eventually through a black mass of pencil lead, he produced sublime letter forms and spacing. Many of the inscriptions you have seen are the work of Lawrence Cribb though they may rightly be signed E. G. This, of course, because we worked in a tradition and the tradition was that of Mr Gill. Yet another contrast between Mr Gill and Laurie was that Mr Gill could not carve animals, but Laurie could. On the other hand Laurie could not carve the human form as well as Mr Gill could. So it came about that Laurie carved and virtually designed the panel of the 'Creation' on The League of Nations

*Short hand memorials to "John Smith." Executed by me for Mr Gill, with unfortunate mistakes, in Hopton-Wood stone.*

*One of many beautifully drawn "Royal Seals," the details being so perfect that the diesinker could but copy without interpretation. (W.A.C.M. Library.)*

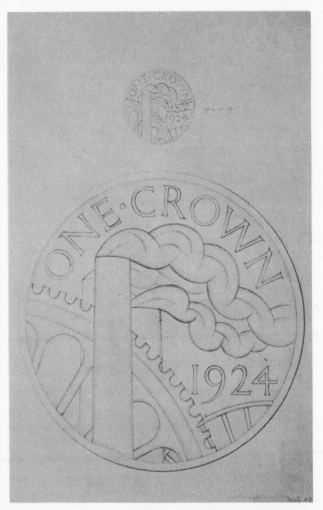

*Designs for coins to coincide with the Wembly Exhibition in 1924. However, the direct reference to industry was not apparently appreciated and these together with numerous other exquisite drawings never became metal. (Drawings in the W.A.C.M. Library.)*

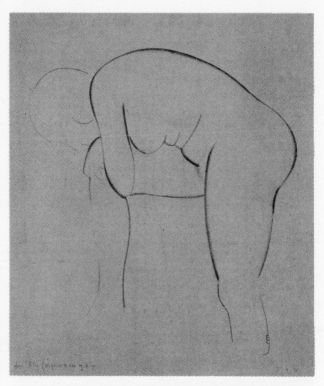

*These fine drawings show clearly how Mr Gill drew from a model. By far the major part of the work was conceived in his mind. The drawing would be worked upon as an image until it became something in itself—not a sketch of hand, eye and dexterity at the moment of seeing. Note the disregard for the direction of light and careful shading on the outside of the form. (W.A.C.M. Library.)*

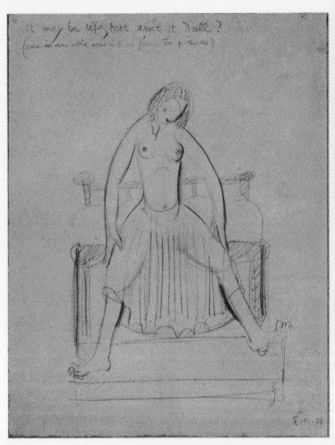

*"It may be life but ain't it dull?"* (*W.A.C.M. Library.*)

Building at Geneva. The main panel was of Man being touched by the hand of God—not an altogether unusual theme amongst painters. It is doubtful if Mr Gill realised this. He certainly designed this magnificent sculpture of man re-awakening as he alone conceived it. "Guess what," he said, with a twinkle in his eye while holding a photograph of the same theme painted by Michelangelo in the Sistine Chapel, "some other bloke thought of this too."

A large block of flats was being put up in London called Dorset House and Mr Gill was asked to design some relief sculpture for the main entrance. The directors were not at all clear what they wanted and left it to the artist to suggest ideas. It was agreed that he would submit designs for the four basic activities that went on in such places—eating, drinking, washing and sleeping. Sleeping and drinking were ruled out though I can't remember why except that his provisional sketches frightened the directors! Even so they found the cost of the remaining two more than they had budgeted for.

Mr Gill was invited to appear before the Board. One member who had heard about Mr Gill's clothes thought he should warn his fellow directors. He explained that he wore a habit similar, though shorter, than a monk's, and being an artist of some distinction he should be treated with due respect. "How could the cost be reduced?" they asked. At once Mr Gill said, "Each leaf is £5, so if you do away with the whole branch that will save £25." The Directors, already bitterly disappointed because Mr Gill had turned up in an overcoat, turned on the one that had thought to smooth the way saying, "He is not an artist. He is a business man. Moreover, we have not seen his monk's habit."

Mr Gill and I worked alone on these carvings late into the night by the light of the street lamps. He talked a great deal to me at that time and with little reserve. I was fascinated by all he said. It was clear that he felt misunderstood and in turn he had misunderstood the contemporary Roman Catholic Church. Though his faith remained firm he was tending more and more to relate his faith to the early Church. It remained a burning shock to him that so much of his belief was unsupported by the Church and what was worse that the Church almost without exception, sanctioned that which he most strongly argued against. His fellow travelling, as the phrase goes, with the communist view of life gained much from his understanding of the early Christians where material things were shared. While he was completely aware of the totally atheistic nature of communism in Russia, he did not view the capitalist system of the West much more favourably. He thought both systems were out to achieve the same materialistic ends and of the two evils he often appeared to favour communism. It was his belief that the modern world, East and West, was predominantly atheistic and that those in power sought by every means of modern technology to seduce the masses of ordinary citizens into accepting a form of slavery that perhaps surpasses anything in the past. These views shocked and stunned my poor stockbroker father. Strangely enough, bricklayers, carpenters and other craftsmen, responded favourably, in spite of the implication of slavery. Those who worked with their hands instinctively admired and were sympathetic with his views, and he always felt a close kinship with the working man.

At Pigotts I sat beside Mr Gill while he was drawing some of the fatter versions of Gill Sans type for Monotype. He could not bring himself to make the necessary changes from his earlier regular version. His original designs were justified in his mind as being fool-proof as regards their mechanical manufacture and capable of being copied by men whose work was mechanical rather than free. But to have to introduce subtlety of a kind that was not easily measurable, would defeat the whole purpose and make a nonsense of his reasoning. "He who pays the piper calls the tune," he said, as he explained to me what was required. Would Mr Gill be proud of the fact, despite all the variations in monoline and sans serif that have been in and out of favour, that his Gill Sans is still found to be much the most legible? Yes, I think he would. He was a first class industrial designer. He knew far better than most of his contemporary artists exactly what one could expect from a machine. He always wanted to know exactly how a machine worked and what was its purpose. For someone who so fiercely challenged the supremacy of machines he took a remarkable interest in their design.

St. John's College, Oxford, commissioned Mr Gill to carve St. John the Baptist for a niche above their Gateway. The honey coloured Clipsham Stone from Rutland slowly revealed the sturdy body of the beckoning John, clad in a skin and holding a strong staff. As I watched and, indeed, helped to find the hidden form, I knew that what was being created was as near to the image in his mind's eye as anything I'd seen him do. His attention was remarkable in degree and duration. No fine tool was used if a coarser one would do the work. No tool was ever forced beyond its capacity. All stages were in process at once on the various parts of the carving. With the projections always a stage ahead it appeared a simple matter of removing a series of skins of differently textured stone. Strength and firmness of form were assured not only by the clarity of his vision but in no small degree by the methodicalness of his technique. All of form for Mr Gill was of a convex order. Concavities were the result of the meeting of two convexities. Bridging pieces of stone were as carefully carved as the rest and vanished as the carving matched its conception, leaving the stone ringing like a bell even if lightly touched. This is one thrill rewarding the carver on the completion of work well done, not always shared by the sculptors of today! Mr Gill had no great compulsion to self expression nor over emphasisation of materials. He did not get involved in the relation of masses. He was not so much a sculptor as a carver, making things in stone which he had conceived in stone.

In the same way he conceived his particular form of dress. Respect for the material was integral with the design and the design was practical. His clothes were well made by a famous firm of tailors and the position of numerous pockets enabled him to produce immediately any requirement of the drawing office, as well as his tobacco and cigarette papers. His skill at rolling a cigarette, with that marked degree of attention he gave the smallest job, was a treat to watch.

Pigotts was altogether an enchanting place. As I have said, it was a rectangular group of buildings around a farmyard, now grown over with grass. There were orchards and a small area of surrounding green fields and then the dense beech woods of Buckinghamshire falling away. Pigotts surmounted the spur of a hill. A narrow lane, capable of only one vehicle at a time, lead precipitously down through the woods to buses and a link with the outside world. It was a haven of peace and sensible occupations. The newcomer was entranced. The visitor left with an indelible impression of a life near to the kingdom of Heaven on earth. The newcomer stayed and, inevitably, some of the vision faded and sometimes vanished. These were people—there were contradictions between the theory and the practice. It could not, of course, be otherwise. Mr Gill was always very busy engraving, carving or writing—preparing talks and, of course, there were letters to the Press. Consequently he did not know the full extent to which the 'farm' intruded on our work. He rebuked Mary, his wife, only occasionally and mildly. Sometimes at Mary's desperate request we fetched the cows back from distant lands. Then the calving became unplanned and spells without milk called for treks down the hill to a neighbourly farmer. Other days we would drive a cow several miles to bull, or hold a cow's tail whilst the vet would search her like a penny dip. All these occupations took up valuable time. Valuable because the workshop earned money and the farm did not. Mr Gill knew this and the odd pat of butter on the table, especially when an important visitor was coming, was somehow not sufficient compensation for all the trials and tribulation. It was a brave but unrealistic attempt to unite the workshop and the farm and a drain on Mr Gill's income that he could ill afford. In this care of the farm the craftsman within Mr Gill seemed blind to the inefficient, amateur husbandry.

There were quite a few blind spots, in fact. One I remember very well caused a lot of amusement. Mr Gill, had a way of arguing himself into impossible positions. He had been invited to dine at The Royal Institute of British Architects. The dinner was in honour of Frank Dobson, another sculptor of the time. I was standing at the foot of the stairs as all these distinguished people came down into the hall to hear Dobson lecture. Mr Gill gave me a broad wink and missed a step. But that is not the point of my story.

Dobson apart from speaking too long—put

forward the theory that man had been interested in 'form' before anything else. Mr Gill could not take this at all. He jumped up to state his counter theory. "Undoubtedly man had first scratched lines long before he was interested in form." "No," said Dobson, "man had undoubtedly rolled up mud and had therefore first been interested in form." So the argument went on and on. Finally, someone pointed out that was it not extraordinary that here were two grown men fiercely disputing something that could hardly be proved either way and interesting in that the scratch theory so exactly fitted Eric Gill's predominantly linear approach to sculpture whilst the mud form theory so aptly fitted Frank Dobson's rounded clay forms. It was still a matter of some importance as we drove back to Pigotts that night!

Mr Gill believed fervently in many causes. He used all the logic he could command in furthering them, combined with a very lucid style of prose. His over-emphasis, perhaps through lack of maturity in early days and later through despair at the way the world was inevitably drifting into war, created for him many critics who otherwise might have been more tolerant of his religious and political views. In my opinion he had the only tenable view of art which was in any way an alterna-

Gordian G.

ЄᏩ

41/50

*A particularly sensitive copper-plate of Mr Gill's son "Gordian."*
*(The copper-plate is in the W.A.C.M. Library.)*

*Original pencil sketch of Beatrice Warde.*

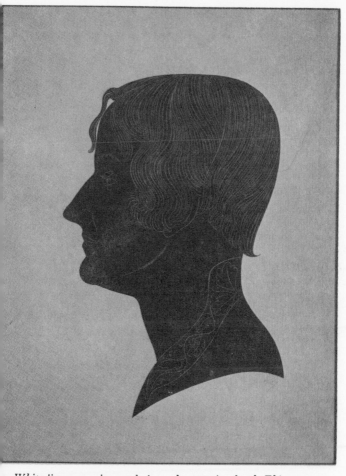

*White line engraving made from the opposite sketch. This was an
early proof, before Gill modified the chin at Beatrice's request.*

*Drawn and painted black ink alphabet. Note the "serifs" felt from the very waist of the letters. (In possession of The University Press, Cambridge. Brooke Crutchley, University printer.)*

*Painted black ink letters, very large. Note flat top on the "A" and serifs on the "C" and short center arm in the "E" and "F". Later Mr Gill invariably drew "E" and "F" within 2 vertical squares with equal length arms. (W.A.C.M. Library.)*

ABCDEFGHIJKLMN
OPQRSTUVWXYZ
abcdefghijklmn
opqrstuvwxyz
abcdefghijklmn
opqrstuvwxyz

*Free wood-block incised line. Illustration in "Typography."*

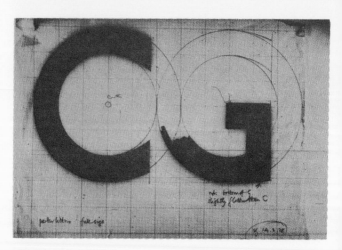

DIEBVS·ISTIS·LOCVTVS·EST
NOVISSIME ...*last of all in these days he has spoken to us by his Son* ........ NOBIS·IN·FILIO
*from Eric & Mary Gill, christmas,1935*

*Friends of Eric and Mary received such beautiful cards as this every Christmas. Freely executed wood-block.*

*Poster letters, with detailed instructions for the signwriter. Cambridge University Press. Brooke Crutchley, University printer.*

*Initial letter enriched with growing leaf so typical of Mr Gill's illustrative work.*

3/5                                    ERIC G

tive to the popular view in the contemporary West. The main springs of his belief were to be found at Chartres and Ajanta through his friend Ananda Coomaraswamy—that great exponent of Indian Art.

Mr Gill's ideas were of a kind that turned the prevailing hypnotic acceptance of Western art completely upside down. "He thought and then he made his thought in stone." He put the intellect at least as high as the emotions. The artist was not a special kind of man but man was a special kind of artist. Anonymity was an ideal and insofar as a work expressed the personality of the maker rather than the subject, it had failed. Such things were either accident or a hindrance to a perfect rendering of an already complete visual concept within the mind.

Meister Eckhart said of the carpenter, who building a house "will first erect it in his mind and, were the house enough subject to his will, then, materials apart the only difference between them would be that of begetter and suddenly begotten." Mr Gill's work was deliberate and intentional—he stood apart from it being simply the executant. He was a balanced man bringing to his work an exceptional intellect, sensitivity and skill. It was in stone that these three were best united. Personally I regret that so much of his energy was encouraged into writing and that no one seems to have adequately suggested to him that we should all have been the more blessed through his stone work and engraving. Indeed, much of his writing, good and apt as it was, is too repetitive.

No one brought more 'grist to his mill' than Coomaraswamy. Although we are apt to think primarily of Mr Gill as Christian and specifically Roman Catholic in his ideals, the impact of Coomaraswamy's introduction to Eastern art was never eclipsed. Indeed, up to a point Chartres and Ajanta were not so far apart. Although Chartres lead him inevitably into the Catholic faith his total being, in my opinion, needed the richer and more sensuous approach of the East. It is sad indeed that so many within the Church piously forced him into interminable argument and defense.

As can be seen in his sculpture, he was a man not 'involved' in the sense popularly understood today. He did not carve in a fury of passion—though he felt as deeply as any. He did not subscribe to any popular 'ism'. He did not know about the relation of masses. He was not aware of any theory of composition. He was not interested in self expression or in expressing the material in which he was working. And above all he was totally at variance with the teaching in art schools. It was not that he was negative to all these things, his system of thought had a quite different source and its fruits were wholly different. Today we are inclined to extol the virtue of total identification with what we are doing. I doubt Mr Gill even considered it a virtue.

I quote from Coomaraswamy's book, *The Transformation of Art in Nature*:

"Our modern system of thought has substituted for this division of labor a spiritual caste system which divides men into species. Those who have lost most by this are the artists, professionally speaking, on the one hand, and laymen generally on the other. The artist (meaning such as would still be so called) loses by his isolation and corresponding pride, and by the emasculation of his art, no longer conceived as intellectual, but only as emotional in motivation and significance; the workman (to whom the name of artist is now denied) loses in that he is not called, but forced to labor unintelligently, goods being valued above men. All alike have lost, in that art being now a luxury, no longer the normal type of all activity, all men are compelled to live in squalor and disorder and have become so inured to this that they are unaware of it. The only surviving artists in the Scholastic, Gothic sense, are scientists, surgeons, and engineers, the only ateliers, laboratories."

I had not long left Mr Gill when the Spanish War broke out. I do not know how you reacted here, but in England none were neutral. We all took sides passionately. Once again Mr Gill fell foul of the majority of the Roman Church. Strongly as he opposed all that General Franco stood for it did not prevent his offering me good advice.

I had been approached by a conservative Member of Parliament about a memorial to commemorate those who were massacred in the Alcazar at Toledo. The Spanish War was still raging and the finished memorial was to be exhibited in London to raise funds for the Franco cause!

As I remember I wrote at some length to Mr Gill asking whether I should accept the commission, and how I felt and what my conscience would have to bear, until my dying day, if I undertook the job.

Mr Gill's reply came by return on a post-card. "Plenty biz. no do! No biz. DO!" It was done.